The Question of Rapture

The Question of Rapture

by Claire Keyes

Mayapple Press 2008

Published by MAYAPPLE PRESS
408 N. Lincoln St.
Bay City, MI 48708
www.mayapplepress.com

ISBN 978-0932412-690

ACKNOWLEDGMENTS

Blueline: The Question of Rapture, Black Bears; *Currents V (Seacoast Writers Association)*: A Little Less Than the Angels; *Crania@digitaldaze.com*: For the Squirrels Nesting in the Attic; *eleventh muse*: Journey to Epidauros, Stranger in Fatigues, Key West Suite; *Embers*: The Granite Boys; *Icon*: Playing Cards With My Father; *Into the Teeth of the Wind*: Nantasket; *Kimera*: Brotherly Love; *Nilas(Nature in Legend and Story)Newsletter*: Samaras, The Feasting of Eagles; *Orbis*: Portrait of Hannah Erdrich-Hartmann and Jana-Marie Hartmann; *Passages North*: Subterranean; *Phi Kappa Phi Forum*: Cliffs of Moher, Hibiscus; *Pleides (Art North)*: Matinee; *Poemeleon.org*: Pieta; *Poetrymagazine.com*: Stranger in Fatigues, Cobb Brook Road, Cliffs of Moher, Gravitation as a Form of Acceleration, Io's Revenge; *Smartish Pace*: Aftermath: The Swans; Sachuest Point, Easter; *Spoon River Poetry Review*: Beach with White Shoe, Io's Revenge; Nauset Beach, October; *Talking River Review*: Bering Seascape; *Tattoohighway.org*: Devereux Beach; Wood, Paper, Poems; *Thema*: Attic Flute; *Wicked Alice Poetry Journal*: Poem Ending in a Line from Sylvia Plath; *Zone 3*: Foreign Movie, Cobb Brook Road; *Anthology of New England Writers '05*: Trespass, '07: Slow Wave; *Heartbeat of New England: An Anthology of Contemporary Nature Poetry*: Cobb Brook Road; *Mercy of Tides: Poems for a Beach House*: Beach with White Shoe; *Key West: A Collection*: Gravitation as a Form of Acceleration. Six of these poems appear in *Rising and Falling*, a chapbook published by Riverstone Press.

My gratitude goes to all my friends-in-poetry who have supported and encouraged me throughout the years. I am especially grateful to Amy Dengler, Regina Flynn, Michelle Gillett, Moira Linehan, Ruth Maassen, Jacquelyn Malone, Betsy Morris and Mary Jane Mulholland. Thanks to the Wurlitzer Foundation in Taos, New Mexico, for believing in me early on. As a member of the Women Poets List-Serv, I have benefited from the knowledge and creativity of my virtual poet-friends who have connected me to a larger world of poetry. And most of all, to Jay Moore.

Cover image by Rose Olson. Cover design by Judith Kerman. Book typset and designed by Amee Schmidt with titles in Monotype Corsiva and text in Californian FB. Author photo by Jana Conway.

Contents

ONE

TWO

THREE

FOUR

For all those I love.

ONE

279 Poplar Street

after a line by Pablo Neruda

One returns to the self
as if to an old house so let the door be open,
let the house smell like clean clothes

you and your mother plucked off lines
in the backyard: shirts, dresses and sheets
the wind had puffed,

leaving a scent of summer leaves
and fields of clover.
Let the sadness of the house fade

the way dreams fade at waking.
Forget your grandfather dying
in the back bedroom, his long groans.

Forget your drunken uncle crawling up the stairs,
your father's anger
swelling and spilling over.

Recall the round wooden table, the family
gathered for supper,
steaming bowls of green beans

and mashed potatoes, the platter of chops,
sliced thin, everyone reaching
at the same time.

Avoid the kitchen filled with dishes
to be washed; it's not your turn.
Your mother has asked you to play the piano

for her and her sister. This time you don't freeze.
Playing *Für Elise*, you enjoy
the rippling notes, the gaiety.

When they applaud and ask for another,
you flip through your music, play and sing
Irish Eyes.

As long as you're returning to your self,
you might as well believe, as they believed,
in your possibilities.

Playing Cards with My Father

My father is shuffling again, the deck split
   in two, his thumbs bending back the cards,

then fanning them like pages in a book. He dices them
   together, deals. It's always late afternoon,

after school, after work, my kid brother and me,
   apprentices to the art of one-eyed Jacks, deuces, trump—

his good buddies for an hour or two.
   I pick up my hand, hold it close to my chest,

as I've been taught, surveying the fanned cards.
   He puffs on his cigar. No joy, no regret,

just a taste for the kill.
   Don't give away anything the other guy can use

to destroy you, even your brother, your father,
   as if kids—I'm ten, Arthur's six—had anything to give away

but luck. We were green as spring clover, as shoots
   of March grass, green and thirsty

for an afternoon with him at the card table, other kids
   reduced to skating on cracked sidewalks, shooting hoops,

playing double dutchies, their chants and rope-slapping
   mere child's play. Another hand, and another.

Don't skunk me, Pop. My mother watches from the kitchen.
   Her game is playing house. With my flair

for the father-tongue, its rules and syntax, I know
   that winning is better than losing.

If you don't have that straight, pretend.
   He takes one card, tucks it into his hand, lifts his eyes.

I'll raise you, he says.

Brotherly Love

My brother sees me once
after months, then crowds my phone,
his protests of love thick in my ears:

Your face is full, says he.
There's something about your fullness.
He probes my health, my weight

as if I possessed a secret he might use
to shame his enemy. And I resist
though his emotion takes me back

over the miles and over the years
when he summoned me to swing high
onto his shoulders. *To be healthy*

is to be beautiful, says he
and his voice soft in my ear:
I love you.

He gets little in return, only
an astonished *Oh!* and my breath
expelled like a long-held wish.

Death must have been pinching him
even then—that tightness near his heart
propelling him to touch me.

And he did, through the distance
we had coolly measured off.
He had a boon to give and he gave it,

allowing me to feel his love as more
generous than a pair of tall shoulders
that meant brother, that giddy height

making me imagine his long arms
said everything about him
I'd need to know.

Journey to Epidauros

That summer in Greece
  we explored the great natural theatre
    of the Peloponnesus: sited against a cliff,
      no roof but the sky, no lights but the sun.

No performance that day, just a climb
  to the amphitheatre's highest seats.
    It's like jumping hurdles: row after row
      of backless stone benches,

the circumference widening until we reach the top
  in a juicy sweat. On stage, our guide
    drops a pin. He's so small and far away,
      I can barely see his hand move, but I can hear

that pin drop, quick and metallic. Beyond it,
  the flutter of queenly robes as Clytemnestra
    advances to greet Agamemnon, his Trojan princess
      by his side, sympathy as foreign to him

as his gorgeous captive, someone else's pain
  an affront to decency. Some can read the gesture
    a hand makes welcoming a husband home
      from the wars, subtle and menacing.

Some flinch at the brilliant rug ordered
  thrown down so the King need not touch his foot
    to the ground. Some never flinch;
      they are too stupid.

            *   *   *

Where it's warmer than Greece can ever be,
  I journey home and push through a series
    of doors: opening, closing, room after empty
      room, until I reach the warmest room of all,

my mother sitting at the table with her sister.
　　They drink tea, always tea, lots of cream,
　　　　two sugars. She rises to greet me, robust and tall
　　　　　as I am, not the shrunken wraith

whose body shook with the death rattle
　　thirty years ago, a sound I hear still
　　　　though it lasted little more than that pin
　　　　　resonating at Epidauros.

What's a mere three decades to a mother and daughter?
　　My mother is plump in my embrace.
　　　　But she's ill, she whispers, and her disease
　　　　　will descend to me and all my sisters

and brothers. I love her arms, her face, her voice,
　　and don't care that she tells a story
　　　　I've heard many times before.
　　　　　I will die. Why brood on this?

Resonance is the stone I throw
　　from the pond's edge to the center.
　　　　First the plunge, then the rings
　　　　　widening and reaching back to shore.

The Cliffs of Moher

Serious cliffs, our Irish friends cautioned,
   Atlantic gusts slamming into the highlands
      on the west coast like some ancient gods
         keen on vengeance. If you must go,

they told us, don't be fools. Some tourists
   flirt with the wind, lean a little too far, find
      themselves flying seven hundred feet to the rocks,
         their cries slammed back into their throats.

At the cliffs, we take a quick scan, watch
   seagulls cruise sideways, tipped as if for disaster,
      the updraft so fierce that tears rip down our cheeks.
         Not a chance we'd tempt these gods.

So we're amazed to see children gather
   in a meadow yards from the edge, arms
      open, the wind belling up their shirts, spilling them
         across the grass, hilarious.

But one small boy huddles next to a shelter,
   crunched into himself, his dad holding out
      his arms. *Come, Nial,* he soothes,
         Don't be afraid.

The child whimpers, his eyes
   riveted on the boys and girls intoxicated
      by the wild play of wind, spinning, falling down,
         picking themselves up.

He wants to be one of them, running,
   laughing, falling, whipped into a frenzy.
      But the terror got there sooner, closer; it licks his ribs,
         a stranger's rude fingers groping and cold.

Slow Wave

(In Ireland, her birthplace, for my mother)

In the butcher's window, hooks
dangle thick legs of lamb. Stone houses
line my mother's street, forbidding

despite their black filigree gates
and curtains of exquisite lace.
Nothing picturesque

in empty lots and piles of rubble;
no family graves
I can discover in the cemetery

among broken tablets, dense shields
of ivy. My grandfather traveled to Spain,
traded horses—and she remembered him

as the hot stench of manure
on a tweed jacket, as a tall shadow on Bishop Street
winter afternoons when she straggled home

from school, the gloom coming on
at half past three like a boozy, wet tongue.
I pocket a few stones, finding in them

that hardness which forged her.
She left, didn't she? Not a timid soul,
nor so soaked in misery

that she didn't take on the Atlantic,
imagining America
not just as a sister's welcoming arms,

but the way a sleeper feels the dawn:
a hint of light through closed lids, then
the slow wave plunging her awake.

Nantasket

My father lights a cigar and opens the newspaper,
wearily telling us to *Go catch a bird*,
meaning *Get lost.*

Was there anything more exotic
than crow or sparrow in the streets of Roslindale?
And how would I have known?

So I got lost instead, danger grabbing me
by the hand, making me believe
I was leading the way

along streets with names familiar as trees:
maple, poplar, birch. But not familiar at all:
the back of a garage, my back pressed against a wall.

Later, I would confess.
Not for nothing had they named me after a saint:
the founder of an order of nuns distinguished

by being poor—and keeping silent. Or maybe
I was named after Uncle Clar who drank too much
and fathered no children,

but he was kind and drove us to the beach
with Aunt Josephine (my middle name), stopping at bars
for—as Auntie explained—*the hair of the dog that bit him.*

I never understood the sense of it,
but I didn't care
as long as we reached the shore,

Nantasket's waves rolling over us, my skin
glowing red, the ocean so frigid
it felt like a burn.

Stranger in Fatigues

The child molester was caught
  in New Hampshire, a man
in black leather, grey hair and boots.

Now everyone knows his little tricks:
  Come to the carnival, little one.
At our place, when the sun ascends

over the trees, the birches stand out,
  their pocked bark. The scrub grows lush
this time of year, raspberry bushes

at every turn. Someone was stealing
  our berries. We imagined the new neighbors
but never the black bear, lifting its snout,

inhaling the blush of red fruit before
  stripping the bushes. When I was a child,
I was fragile inside despite legs

like an elegant colt. The stranger in fatigues
  noticed. Is it easy to violate children?
Those Concord kids ran away and told

their parents who told the police
  who found the man who swears he's innocent,
a lover of Keats and Kerouac.

He teaches English at some exclusive school
  and detests everyone,
the paper says, except children.

Devereux Beach

If I remain parked here long enough, facing the beach.
If the waves roll in to crash in foaming curls, the sea
gray-blue and inviting only to a dog who dares the surf,
then skitters back, playing its own game. If raindrops
hit the windshield, then slide down, slick-silver ribbons.
If I listen to Celtic music on the radio and think of my mother,
just a girl crossing this same ocean when the only way out
of Ireland was by sea. If it's still that girl—fatherless at six,
motherless at ten—who engages me: that thirteen year-old
lady's companion, her passage paid. If she was pushed
to approach the unknown, resisted, shook its hand, shivered.
If she was brave. I don't know. If I'm now a year older
than she was when she died: matron, wife, mother of eight.
If the mind insists on imagining its origins, then it comes
to this wintry beach, waves pulsing towards shore.

Portrait of Hannah Erdrich-Hartmann and Jana-Marie Hartmann

—Thomas Struth, 1987

An interior shot, a curtained window to the side, nothing else
exposed in the room but the juxtaposition of heads and shoulders:

mother, daughter. Jana-Marie leans into her mother's solid form,
loose and relaxed in a scruffy sweatshirt, its neck hole pulled wide,

the number eleven sinuous in the shirt's generous folds.
She drapes her arm across Hannah's shoulders, fingers cupped

softly against her mother's neck. She is four or five.
Hannah's cable-knit allows glimpses of blouse through the darkness

of its open weave, her collar neat against her lined neck.
No one can see through that face. She could be thirty.

She doesn't smile. Jana-Marie almost smiles, the edges of her mouth
turning up. It excites her to pose for Struth; anything new excites her.

She is a child, her face cherubic, her blonde hair an unruly mass
succumbing to a braid drifting over her left shoulder. Her mother

has smoothed and fixed her dark waves behind her neck.
She doesn't fuss with hair. No Madonna, she suspects Struth

sees something she doesn't want seen. The child is the self uncontained,
eager to pour its being into the camera's lens. She thinks a stranger's gaze

is a mode of love, that love will envelop her, like a mother's caress,
all of her days, that it will never demand more than she is able to give.

18

King Snake

On my walk this morning, a king snake, the tip of its tail
crushed by a passing car. It bled on the macadam

and twitched, a bad dream. When I was a child
something stark and evil struck me. It left a scar, long

as a snake and crimped at the edges. No one can protect you
from pain, says the scar. Macadam black as pitch and a straight

yellow line. For sure, it would become road kill, just another lump
some driver would flatten while flicking ash from a cigarette.

I looked again: at the snake, at Vermont hills—soft and full;
down to the brook running under the bridge. No trolls. No traffic

to halt me from moving the snake on the hood of my shoe
into the grass where it shook free, where the grass parted and closed.

Attic Flute

Other children poking tarbubbles or casting stones
and jumping into chalked-off squares, summer half-gone,

you, alone in the attic surrounded by boxes of old shoes, galoshes
and figure skates, flaps open, laces stolen. The sheen

of a silvery flute at the bottom of a box: what you came for, abandoned
your friends for. You stroke its contours and purse your lips,

blowing into the topmost hole as if you could will fingers, breath,
lips into a magical configuration that says music, says song.

All you produce is naked sound, its dress missing, a poor shivering thing.
You toss the flute back in the box to watch dust motes dancing

in a shaft of light. And so jubilant the dance, so various its chaos
there's no boredom, no distress. Squinting at roof lines

out the window, you alter their shapes, planes of one shifting
into another, breaking into a shimmer. You keep your magic to yourself,

cracking the window to hear your friends playing hide and seek
in the backyards, their cries wafting over the houses—

allez, allez, all-en-free . . .

TWO

Trespass

The hairy man lazes in the brook, his back
    sloped against a rock. He is naked
      the way the brook is naked

in its rush to get to the foot of the mountain.
    Dusk gathers evening into dark pockets.
      The man grins to himself.

Only family and friends allowed in the brook,
    his neighbor had announced.
      He allows his buttocks to shift

against the rock, lifts a foot to watch water
    trickle down his leg. *Allowed*:
      like she was a priestess and this land

her temple. So he timed his immersion, knowing
    about her walks with the sleek black lab.
      How delicious to be caught:

the dog prancing on the bank, yelping.
    And the man is naked and hairy
      and she is forced to look at him

in his slithery nakedness.
    He loves the transparency
      of her face, the twist of heel,

the great intimacy of her anger, how
    she pulls him into herself, despite herself.
      And he will never go away.

The Question of Rapture

Mid-September and a troop of girls passes me,
riding single file—*clip-clop, clip-clop*—

black helmets bobbing, lovely fawn jodhpurs
pressed tight against horses' flanks.

Their cry—*There's a moose!*—
electrifies the air, as if a demon had appeared among them.

The moose charges across Kellogg's pasture, then angles
onto the road, head lifted, his nostrils wide

with the keen smell of horse. He seems an emanation
of the woods, his desire ignited in the forest

along with the burnished red and gold of the maples.
Cantering to join them, a grandeur of shoulders

slendering to agile hips, he's enraptured
by all those swaying haunches, the girls' shrieks

sending him towards me, only witness to his chagrin.
Hooves pounding, head swinging as if embarrassed

at desire so rudely deflated, he clambers back
through the brush. Then it is at least as quiet

as the sun pulling away from the earth, vacant
as the word *alone* pressed into the road by the slap-slap

of my sneakers. *Alone, alone*
until I pass those foolish girls and break into a run,

my feet gobbling up the road.
Oh rapture, now where will you go?

Foreign Movie

—for Luigi Pirandello

All we know is the family
from Sicily going to join their father in exile
in Malta. No wind. A peaceful island.
Children in their underwear—three girls
and a boy—climb a mountain of pumice.
Its surface crumbles to powder,
but the base is solid enough to grab.

Below them, on a blanket, their mother rests
from the sea voyage, her head cradled
in her oldest daughter's lap. To the side,
a sailor-guardian stands watch. The girl
seems content as she comforts her mother, but
her eyes wander to the children scrambling up
the mountain. The camera lingers on the mother

as she studies her daughter's face.
You want to go? the mother says. The girl nods
a reluctant yes, then strips to lovely, old-fashioned underwear.
She thinks she can recapture what has fled, but her hips
and breasts won't let her. She jiggles as she runs
and the sailor watches as she crawls up the hill.
Now all the children are covered with dust.

When they tumble down to the sea, we watch them
in a long shot from the top of the mountain, our breaths
caught in the cups of our throats. As if they could swim
all the way to Malta, they elbow the waves, their heads
and arms bobbing up and down. The camera never returns
to the woman on the blanket and I miss seeing her
struggle to her feet, motherly antennae aquiver.

But I know why the artist resists closure,
why we accept the island simply as interval:
it's that moment between moments
when exile is nothing, not even terrible.

The Granite Boys

No rails anymore, no trains just a path through the woods
and up ahead two boys in school jackets sitting on slabs of granite,

nothing to do except be nowhere where anyone can see them.
To beat me to the asking, the taller one pulls a box of cigarettes

out of his pocket as he locks eyes and mumbles, *How you doin'*?
But I say nothing, thinking about boys who play hooky

and how they write *Suck* huge & black on ex-curbstones
and then sit on it when someone passes by.

Huck Finn had an island for the hiding and a raft
to navigate the Father of Waters with fatherly Jim.

He'd shun this place tamed by walkers and joggers,
then made crazy by maniacs who labor under the bridge

spray-painting Swastikas, preferring Belsen to Auschwitz—
easier to spell. Broken glass, trash. *THE WHO?* looking gentle

beside *Skinheads.* Images of boys with closely-shaved hair.
See my skull. See the tattoos on the back of my head.

My boys of the granite slabs sport no tattoos, not yet.
And where can they run except into my head and out again.

How you doin'? How am I doing? Not so well, not so whole
that I can fit you into my morning—leaves blazing, berries ripened.

Birds flicker across my path, then you boys, sullen and furtive.
You're no kids of mine, no kin, no one I know—or would admit

knowing. Dirty boys writing filthy things in hidden places.
You're the dream that shocked me awake, the hot need I curb

—or relish

Nothing Vicious

Because I dropped by for the Sunday papers,
   Mr. Jakes came to recognize me,

wrote my name on a register slip. And I came
   to recognize him, gray hair slicked back

and caught in a rubber band, arms laced with tattoos,
   nothing vicious: an anchor, a small snake

spiraling down from the sleeve of his Harley t-shirt.
   Did he notice that I noticed?

Always his entourage: men in overalls
   and railroad caps hanging out by the counter,

giving me a what-have-we-here look
   when Mr. Jakes hands over my *Sunday Times*

and *The Globe. That'll keep you busy*, he says.
   I pocket my change, read *B-A-D* emblazoned

on his forearm. Because his manner is austere
   and fine, what is bad in him summons me,

a summons I might heed or resist, I'm not sure,
   returning again and again: papers, bread . . .

Subterranean

When I dream of the man I used to love, we ride
the train back home. Smoking a cigarette, he gazes out
the night window at his reflection. He can see me

in the shadow behind his back as I hand over
my ticket. He can't find his. Walking away, I smile.
What am I supposed to do? At the station

when I turn around to see if he might follow,
he curses and shakes his fist. And I remember why
I fell for him in the first place. A man of passion,

what a thrill. Even as I walk toward the exit,
I fix his image like some saint on a holy card,
the uplifted eyes, the arrows piercing his breast.

*

Last night, waking to find you beside me,
I kissed the soft place on your shoulder, listened
to the pulse of your breath. I've tried to tell you

about those I've loved, but you don't want to hear.
How can I hide the hands that have held me? I teach them
to you and you sleep much sounder than I ever can,

your fears more open. For the trip we've planned,
you imagine my complaints about the food
and hard mattresses, my heart given to a hitchhiker

I find too handsome to resist.
Slipping back into sleep, I want to dream again
about that train, though its rumble grows fainter,

the fare harder to pay. Dreaming and waking,
I like the play of tension I feel, the tug.
No one I've loved can ever leave me.

Pieta

It never happened like this.
Mary's beauty is young, her brow pristine,
her adult son draped across her knees,

his body blending seamlessly into hers.
She slips her hand beneath his right shoulder,
adjusts that ponderous weight, his head

thrust back, ghastly ribs pronounced.
On her lips, serene containment.
No unseemly howls of grief, no gnashing of teeth

as her son stiffened into a corpse.
Marble, smooth and white as an elephant's tusk,
denies Calvary's filth, its blood and spit.

For the sculptor, death is simply material;
the reality of it so mundane, so temporal
that he erases it.

Beach with White Shoe

Poised on a high stretch of beach
   where the tide won't pull it back
into the surf, a single white shoe

gapes open on the sand to remind me
   of the sweetness
contained in ordinary things,

the poignancy of their loss. And of beaches
   where shoes flung onto the sand
were attached to the feet and legs

of men who cast themselves from ships.
   My brother at twenty-one.
Who killed. Who took shrapnel

in the gut. Who looked his enemy
   in the eye and prayed
not to be killed. Who gave thanks

when he was left bleeding in a ditch.
   Back home, he showed us his Purple Heart.
I didn't know what it meant,

could only stare in horror that summer
   at the beach
when he wore those skinny trunks

and I saw the sudden cave in his belly,
   the humps where thread knit
the edges of his flesh.

What if I need a single shoe
   to remind me of Jim
and the question he asked me:

why did Daddy let me go to war?
   As if I knew,
as if anyone could have held him back.

Sanctus

At the altar boy's flare, tall white spires ignited,
my prayers as ardent as the peasants' prayers
in the print that hung in my parents' house:
the clear, pure sound of *The Angelus*

chiming over the fields, church bells too potent
and lovely to ignore. Of course, I left it—the splendor
of Sunday mornings and High Mass, rich brocaded vestments,
baroque censers swinging pungent incense, the choir

sweeping down the aisles. Left those weekdays in the chapel,
quiet and dim as a cave, women in their stout winter coats
and kerchiefs, old men bent into their dreadful coughs,
stifled for the *sanctus, sanctus, sanctus.*

At the altar rail, head lifted, eyes shut, I was a baby bird,
the brittle thinness of the communion wafer on my tongue
—*not to be chewed*, Sister said—as if bread so fine
would simply melt. Suddenly, my body was stretching

taller, fuller—by no will of my own, its rhythms daring me
not to notice. I thought to do other things—read Lawrence
and Woolf, spend the summer in Greece, ride with my lover
to obscure beaches. Yet when the sun pierced the clouds,

daggers of light flung down to earth, I recalled the host
lifted high, the words: *Take this and eat* as the bells rang
once, twice, three times. Then the heady silence
in which God appeared, unseen but felt as a tingling

along the spine, a shudder, then a loss too terrible for speech.

A Little Less Than the Angels

My brother doesn't read books,
    except for the *Bible*, his choice
        even before his wife became his baby,
           slumped in her wheelchair,

rolling her tongue around her gums
    as if searching for missing teeth.
        And who is he smoothing her hair,
           pressing a cup of water to her lips?

He points to tracks he's rigged
    along the ceiling, the pulleys he's attached
        so he can lift her from wheelchair
           to toilet to bed, careful to tuck her knees,

her feet, checking her eyes for signs
    of comfort or distress. Evenings,
        he pedals his stationary bike and reads
           the Psalms, reciting them over and over

to keep from falling asleep. Because
    it's tiresome and lonely, though
        he doesn't complain. Weekdays,
           he escorts her to day-care, staying

to play the banjo and sing tunes
    for the old ladies who nod and tap their feet.
        Let me call you sweetheart, they sing along,
           making eyes at him, loving him so much

they want to take him home.
    My brother is a lover. He presses fifty pounds
        on the shoulder machine at the Y,
           bathes his wife three times a week

and needs his strength so she doesn't slip
    from his arms. Then what would he do
        to Praise the Lord, all He hath given,
           all He hath taken away?

Amazing Grace

You taught me pleasure has its grace: the dance
between us as we walked, your joyful glance;
your shoulder pressed against my shoulder, your hip
finding its way to mine; your love a courtship
as savory as wine, as pleasing. Mornings—
your place or mine, a cappuccino, rumpling
your hair, your curls so black. I warmed an egg
between my palms and never thought you'd renege
on your kisses, teach me pleasure has its hazards:
a knife left unsheathed, a bed with shards
of glass between the sheets. To live with less
than you was summer with no sun, duress
I had to weather on my own. And then,
bereft of pleasure, I learned I wanted it again.

Balcony Scene

He turns away from her to the orchestra
so engrossed is he in the passage of Haydn's theme,
its delicate inversions as it moves from cello to viola.

She crosses her legs, ignored—and bored to the extreme.
Uncrossing her legs, she tilts her ankle, propelling
her skirt farther above her knees. It must seem

so dreary to her, the maestro's music as compelling
as a Baptist hymn, the conductor's eloquent hands
less potent than the tilt of her lover's chin, less telling.

No longer young (neither is he), she makes demands
on his attention, wedging her shoulder against his,
her need so poignant, her desire so hot it expands

across the rows. Something about how she is
here but not here. Something almost desolate
in her desire. Surely this marriage of mistress

and Haydn is a colossal blunder. Distracted, yet
alert, he rests his palm on her thigh, her panty
hose slick and shiny, and caresses her as if to forget

he plans to jilt her. For which there's scanty
evidence once we've applauded, slung on our coats
and he turns to assist her, leaning over, jaunty

yet devoted. Despite how wrong she is, how she gloats
as her mink slides onto her shoulders, he brushes
his lips against her cheek and she rises, she floats!

Nauset Beach, October

How admirable the waters looked,
   waves surging in, collapsing on shore
and the two of us strolling by.
   It's summer no more though the air is warm,

the sky blue. My lover adores the surge
   beneath him, so he strips to his trunks
and flings himself into the surf. How blue
   his skin turned and how he shivered

in my arms as I tried to warm him, drawing
   my jacket around him. No lips ever seemed
so blue. Passersby on the sand paused
   and clucked, noting my fine hands

stroking his shoulders. It's not every day
   I'm the madonna, the man on my knees
shivering and blue. After this, I loved him less
   and tried to pretend I loved him more.

A man so mad for the ocean might throw himself
   into anything and then how much comfort
would I be expected to give? Yet
   he was once my blue ocean. I threw myself

into his surge. Blue is the color of chagrin.
   Once I held a man unclothed and shivering
on my knees. The sky was blue and Nauset Beach
   felt as solid under our foot soles

as the love we wrapped our legs around each night,
   so drunk with ourselves that we never noticed
the time like a fine blue wave lifting its head
   to see how much longer to shore.

Bering Seascape

First, the half-dead whale flung onto the curved beach.
Then the great huffings of the bear, the relentless thump

of its paws, its grizzled-brown fur spectral among the ice floes.
Fog hides the splitting open of flesh: incisors, tongue,

stupendous claws, the curl of steam as organs burst open
and blood froths from wounds. He eats from the inside out,

ignoring the raven's black stabs of craving, the gulls
driven to wild careenings, their wings flogging the air

with the petulance of need. Stuffed with blubber and whale-guts,
the whale's generous hide as coverlet, the bear collapses into sleep.

Then the people come: skinny heads, flailing arms. One stretch
will do, a clacking of teeth. The grizzly settles back, the suck

and pull of the tide rippling into his sleep, his body wreathed
with scarves of fog twisting up and around his bloody snout.

At Sachuest Point, Easter

Where shelves of rock descend farthest
into the sea, mergansers
patrol the shallows, winter guests

who are avid connoisseurs
of small, slippery fishes.
The lone male, his head feathers

unmistakably rakish
and tilted, is handsome
but blasé as I am: my wishes

for Easter baskets, for some
chocolate chicks and pink eggs
having long faded and become

simply childish craving, the last dregs
of pagan myth. The surf creams
and whispers as if it begs

to differ. Granite rock seems
solid yet jagged cracks split
ledge from ledge. Likewise, my dreams

of a divine savior held strong, their permit
to crumble long delayed. The big old Easter
moon remains. Late last night

it flooded the shore line, *her*
moon, the moon of the goddess
Eos. Its bright curvature

signals rebirth and fullness,
the splendor of spring waiting
to be seen, and, perhaps, to bless.

Black Bears

At the far edge of the clear-cut,
  shifting black shapes come
    into focus—a mother bear

and two cubs—spooked
  by the rude clatter my boots make
    on the gravelly road, their color

the color of midnight in this latitude,
  moon hung with clouds,
    sky free of stars.

The little ones shimmy up
  a towering red pine, then
    cling to the tree

like a bad case of nerves,
  the mother lumbering off
    into the bushy woods.

She turns to gauge the threat
  I pose to the cubs, curious
    as any fine young animals

at what moves so fearlessly
  along the trail—fair-haired, pale-
    skinned, long arms and legs,

walking upright—lacking the grace
  of a deer, too compact
    for a moose. They can hear

the huffings of my breath
  as I walk fast then faster, body
    stiff, arms swinging. I avoid

their gaze, keep moving
  like someone who knows nothing
    about being entranced.

For the Squirrels Nesting in the Attic

They can't remember
how they found this incredible trove—what crevice
in the shingles finally gave way

to a maze of timbers and fabulous pink fluff.
Every day of that dreadful winter,
the distant rumble of the furnace

ticked on, predictable as dawn
and their screaks grew less anxious.
Were they not among the blessed

in this attic warmth? Mounds of stuff,
flung here and forgotten, sunlight flashing
through air vents, provoking dust motes

into slow-dancing. One nestles
in a hat box, her tail tucked under her snout,
her sleep dreamless.

Isn't this space the stash of stashes?
Between naps and quick forays for food,
they chase each other around

stacks of books, boxes of slick magazines;
skis, boots, poles. On midnight gambols
behind sheetrock, they enter the zone

of rhythmic snores and sweet, easy breathing.
And what happens to their bodies
inside those bedroom walls?

Claws retreat, tails slender
to a dash and they're pure energy,
the insanity of delight.

THREE

A Minor Nation

At twilight on our porch, I listen as crickets serenade,
males wooing females, a chorus both loud and constant.

A charmed evening: no need for the slap of fans, wet leaves
glistening after a welcome wash of rain. Inside the screen door,

the ebb and flow of Sox fans cheering/jeering a late season
ballgame, the banter of gritty baritones noting the play.

From the grass, strings of sound swell to fortissimo.
To listen is to feel the poignancy of this season.

From the couch, a *whoop! hoo!* of joy as the bat's sweet spot
attracts the ball. It's a grand slam. Meanwhile, the crickets

pursue their own game and when the females respond,
what silence, what accord. In time, the gods do listen.

Samaras

While you are gone, it rains seeds
from the maples: tiny green wings
slanting down

to the ground
like arrows to a target.
Nothing will stop them.

They sheathe the car, work themselves
inside the trunk and engine, carpet
the driveway.

I push them into mounds,
gather them up, thrust them away.
More descend.

In the sweet caves of underbrush,
seedlings flourish. I pull up ten-inchers
invading the compost heap, flower beds,

cracks between bricks.
It's too much, I tell you
on the phone, meaning everything

that overwhelms when you're not here.
You tell me those green wings
are called *samaras,* your voice

cupped close inside my ear,
samaras suddenly intimate
and thrilling.

Matinee

The pianist thrusts open the lid of the Steinway,
a slender stick to brace its jaws. I slip my coat
off my shoulders, black wool sleeves slump
and deflate. You study the program beside me
like a stranger, eyes lowered. Notes cascade
into other notes: music, I decide, means nothing

but itself. Cellist and violinist gesture
with eyebrows. Chins lift. I imagine you not here
but home watching the game on TV; you luxuriate
on the couch. Do you nod off? Do you snore?
All the sounds you make are music to me.
Matinees fill a vacuum, Mendelssohn and Brahms

killing a winter Sunday afternoon. I follow
the pianist's hands; eloquent male fingers chase,
capture and release sounds. The audience rises to applaud;
feet shuffling, stiff fingers striking palms.
You rise beside me, our shoulders brush. The musicians
smile and bow, leaning over together, three black backs.

On the stairway, an usher hands me a red flower,
a Valentine's Day carnation: someone loves me.
We walk outside to sunset and slush, boots stepping
in rhythm through snow. Slipping my arm through your arm,
I slide my hand into your pocket. The sky tonight
is like nothing we've ever seen, gray lowering clouds,
a slim margin of pink.

Winterscape, Boston

A scruffy man holds out his hand,
  his cap pulled low.
We pretend we don't see him,

and enter the Public Garden,
  its pond slabbed with ice.
Hardy mallards skid down the banks

to forage in pools of snow-melt.
  The sun is making its slow descent,
each day a little longer, a little sweeter

as winter recedes. A woman tosses
  peanuts for squirrels, anxious
behind elms whose leggy shadows

pattern the snow. My arm in yours,
  we walk through the Common,
through the shadows, descend underground

where the crowd swirls, coagulates,
  then breaks into pieces.
Their homes are elsewhere, mine with you.

On the Green Line, we thread
  the labyrinth of bodies, grab a hold
and sway as the trolley pitches forward,

my shoulder touching yours, the city
  and its sly gestures folded
into our coats, on our bootsoles,

ringing in our ears as the car screeches
  to a stop, then lurches back,
the city not willing to let us go.

Hibiscus

Freed from winter sidewalks sheeted with ice, we revel
in the heat and the hibiscus blooming along roadways

south of Miami: not the brash red of a stop sign, but cheek-flush,
that pink. While you drive, bemused, I wriggle into shorts,

slough off shoes and socks. Once again, maybe forever . . . toes
naked as Eden. *I like to sweat*, you tell me. It reminds you of summers

on the shore, your father home from the war. You promised me
the Everglades and I imagined something lush and Amazonian,

not the browned flatland we cruise by car, driving from waterhole
to waterhole, alligators lying near the surface, their scaly backs

like old logs floating in the shallows. They fool me every time, until
I catch an eyeball shifting, a snout yawning as if to say, *what luscious toes*

you have, my dear, what generous cheeks. Backing off, I will myself
to think of hibiscus, its frills defining edge, its fragile insouciance.

Gravitation as a Form of Acceleration

Driving all the way from Massachusetts
to Key West, we didn't fight
until we hit the outskirts of Miami,
having it out in a food court
in a shopping mall—you eating the liver
and onions I refuse to cook at home
while I explain verbal abuse and devour
my teriyaki chicken, certain

our staying together is something
more compelling than inertia: like
finding ourselves strolling from north to south
along the narrow streets of Key West,
admiring the creamy porches, filigree gates,
the way the ocean opens up
clear to Cuba, our rental house
cooled by February breezes, its windows
flung open, bushy trees rising to roof level
with jets flying over so low
you might leap up and touch a wing,

and because our next-door neighbors
hammer hour after hour on their addition,
their cats selecting our patio
for evening strolls, mewling pitifully
as if they've not been fed since birth—
we retire early
and because we sleep in a strange bed
wide enough for three
(*Not good for marriages*, you say),
we gravitate most naturally
towards the center.

Key West Suite

1. On Truman Avenue

It's easy to be lazy here
behind tropic bushes, frangipani,
bougainvillea, our rental house
leaning beside its sisters, cream-
white, with filigree porches and busy
ceiling fans, the steady beat
of traffic fading to a hum
on the avenue. We curve into the sun.

The parrot next door
pokes a hole in our idle chatter.
Uh, oh, he says behind bushes
as if warning us we might trip
and fall into the pool or burn
if we don't shift out of the sun.
For revenge, we spy on him,
white people in shorts peeking through
thick bushes at a shock
of green and red, a breast
yellow enough for banana.

> I say, *Pretty boy.*
> He says, *Uh, oh.*

2. Next Door

Behind the bushes, I hear women talking.
They can't see me lounging beside the pool
where their voices blend with street noise
and the songs of warblers arriving daily
from South America. Butterflies float
among the bougainvillea, their wings flapping
like silken sleeves. Needles click.
A man walks by in blue shorts
and a green shirt, no sleeves.
He is eating something. It must be good.
Everything tastes good here, sounds good.
Even the clatter of the big truck

spilling garbage into its back.
If we're lucky, the osprey will fly over
on its way to its nest. A woman humming
ascends the stairs.

3. *Key Deer*

If I possessed eyes like hers,
wide and solemn, I'd trust edges less.
She pauses near the road,
then lifts her nose, ears primed.
Wind spills through tall pines.
You say, *Hush.* We freeze in place.
Turkey vultures soar above Big Pine Key,
their circles hungry, great broad wings
vicious against the blue sky.
The deer feeds on leaves, crosses the road.

4. *A Spray of Orchids*

I nap beside the pool and you flick me
with your bright wings, butterfly wings
that last no longer than youth lasts.
Friend of my youth, you wore your charm
like a spray of orchids. Your laughter
danced around us; no one was loved like you.
In my dream, I follow you along gray walls
and into rooms where glass thickens
like layers of pain, scenes of anguish
I'd as soon leave behind. Sleep is so easy here.
You told me you never sleep,
that you can't lie still for the pain
that occupies your body as if it had the right.
They cut into your brain
to take out the voices, but voices taunt you still
as if they had the right.
You wanted only what was yours
and mine: those pearls that gleam
like bright stars beneath the water.
Shaking myself awake, I breathe deeply
and dive where shadows float
careless as dreams.

Aubade with Papaya

Key West porches wrap around
  themselves; only sunlight necessary
to shift butterflies from slumber

to the pink lip of the hibiscus. In dawn's
  pale blue sky, a less-than-half moon
rides above a plane beginning its descent,

rattling my teacup like a wave of anxiety,
  then anxiety appeased. The precise whisper
of palm fronds shifting in the breeze,

wind-chimes adroit in response. The papaya
  about to drop from its stem, fragrant
and yellow as sin. To think I could have

missed all this, curled up in bed, my hand
  resting on my husband's thigh, dreaming
of papayas, reaching for one golden on the branch:

  most golden, most unreachable.

Key West Cemetery

Where the dead are not buried
in the ground but on the surface,
marked by granite or marble
monuments, they are never
fully forgotten, the cemetery
a destination for walkers and tourists.
Sailors and officers of *The Maine*
are buried here (Remember *The Maine?*),
the whole array of tombstones funky
in a Key West funky kind of way:
the jaunty airplane for the fellow
who loved to fly, the sly quip,
I told you I was sick.
And the poignant marble
Tim brought me to see that hot day
sweat trickled down our faces
and he told me the story of the girl
raped, her throat slit, a bust difficult
to find, impossible to forget:
the uplifted head, the smooth
and gracious arc of her neck.

FOUR

Wood, Paper, Poems

You promised me a pretty lake
if we chose this path sprinkled with wildflowers:
flagrant reds, champion blues, but how subtle
was Allied Lumber with its backhoes
running giant claws across the mountain,
leaving behind this tangled slash
of branches, twigs and stumps?

A scavenger with a chain-saw and a pick-up
works at the slash, reducing it to chunks
he can burn or sell. He gives us a nod as we pass
in our sturdy boots, their thick rubber treads.
I'm reminded of the pilgrim in the hallowed book
snapping a twig from the tree, falling back
when the tree speaks:

Why do you break me?
Have you no pity then?

Ravaged, I lament,
and there's more slash ahead.
I don't want to see it, want to turn back to camp.
Only you won't let me. After the clear-cut,
a stupendous view, a panorama.
Where do you think wood comes from
anyway? Wood, paper, poems?

Cobb Brook Road

Unimproved they call it, meaning
  a dirt road absent of traffic
    so we can stop smack in the middle

and contemplate two skinny shadows
  cast by a gibbous moon.
    Night light, silver. Not a single cloud.

No noise but a puff of wind rifling
  tall branches. A hermit thrush rises up
    to complain, then a hush so deep

we can measure our wealth: a clutch of land
  in the backwoods, such gracious solitude
    we almost feel guilt. Tonight

we go off-road, down the path
  shaped by spring melt to the brook.
    Stretched out on the bank

as if weary of holding up the world,
  two maples blown down in winter storms.
    We sit on them and listen

to white water splash over bedrock
  as it has since the last glacier slid north,
    no pause for revision, no pause for doubt.

Nest

How foolish to build the nest where he would mow;
how foolish to mow; how else to keep the trees,
ferns, and bushes from taking over the meadow.

The nest enfolds three sky-blue eggs and he's
filled with chagrin, though he didn't hurt
anything. Fern fronds wave in the breeze

and he takes a few, hoping to convert
them to nest-cover, the sheltering grasses
shorn. Retiring to the porch, his T-shirt

soaked with sweat, he contemplates masses
of gray clouds tumbling over the hills
engulfing patches of blue. In what passes

for nonchalance, he lifts the paper, fills
his gaze with the day's news, blocking the view
of the meadow, half-mown. As sunlight spills

through the clouds, the thrush, as if on cue,
touches down on the grass, approaches the nest
then flies away. He lowers the paper, no clue

she'd come or whether she'd return, no interest
in finishing his task. Tomorrow, next week,
if he can stomach it, he'll check the nest.

Io's Revenge

While you train the scope on the night sky,
   searching millions of miles away
for Jupiter, I fill you in on my favorite moon,

named for some lovely and obscure Greek girl.
   All she did was refuse sex
with the king of the gods and look what happened:

yoked to him for eternity, a piddling moon
   to his magnificent planet.
On earth, she had it worse, the god's wife

transforming her into a cow, a cloud of flies
   ordered to nip at her cheeks,
flanks, heels. In spite, Jupiter gave her death

and the sea nestling Greece and its islands, Ionian
   waves slapping the shores of Asia Minor.
In the scope we see tiny dots dance into focus,

then rampant, anarchic flaring. *Let him have it*,
   I chortle when comets bombard Jupiter,
fiery showers I liken to Io's revenge

as they implode in the planet's sizzle and my tongue
   finds a home in a universe so amazing
and lethal I have to belong here.

The Feasting of Eagles

Like mourners expecting to inherit, the eagles
wheel into the trees around the lake's shallow end,

missing nothing about the glut of salmon, eggs laid,
their desperate *pock-pock* as they lift their heads.

Vultures circle, patterning a V for vigilance.
Fish are dying to procreate and it's all right

to loathe the eagles as they swoop to seize
a plump silver brilliance and ferry it to a tree.

Even so, we thrill to the whoosh of their wings,
shrinking back under the shadow of their magnificence,

noting the gobbets of flesh splatting onto earth.
That rustle in the brush is coyote. It's a love-feast,

even the eagles refusing to squabble. Only the ravens flap,
their rude *crawk-crawk* echoing through the woods.

Falling Fire

> *Too pretty dreamlike mimicry!*
> *O falling fire and piercing cry*
> *and panic, and a weak mailed fist*
> *clenched ignorant against the sky*
> *—Elizabeth Bishop*

Too pretty dreamlike mimicry!
The forget-me-nots seize the garden
blue upon blue, even poking up
in cracks near the garage, May's
insurgent offering to the bumblebee.
Too pretty, dreamlike mimicry!

O falling fire and piercing cry
far from this placid neighborhood.
Today's carnage: four marines in a Hum-Vee
an *explosive device*, their blood pooling,
their bodies shattered, all awry.
O falling fire and piercing cry

and panic, and a weakened male fist
jammed hard against his teeth, the sole
survivor, not wanting to cry—or live—
if this be the price: his buddy's head cradled
in his arms, crushed. For the man death missed,
panic and a weakened male fist

clenched ignorant against the sky
that is bluer than blue today, clouds
blown away like so much fluff. Then
sirens, medics, the chopper hovering
for its gruesome cargo—four corpses lie
clenched against the ignorant sky.

Now the Bright Summer

A butterfly cruises the porch, settles
on grass-stained socks. *It's drawn to the scent
of human sweat*, you tell me, stripping off

your shirt, dropping the newspaper, its headlines
too grim for afternoons drunk with the sun,
the cicada's hot insistence.

More people killed in the Middle East,
a mother, her three children.
There's nothing we can do about it.

In a darkened room, a young man
tapes a bomb to his chest, on his face
an expression so quiet and serious

he might be sitting for an exam at school.
He flattens his shirt, zips his jacket.
Never in his life has he felt so pure, so devout.

A café in the city. A market where fruits are displayed
in luscious rows. A checkpoint. Pieces of flesh.
A child's hand.

Far from terrorists and cowardly bombs,
our cabin boasts a hard red door, a tin roof
where rain beats down in sudden mountain storms.

Beyond these hills, quiet houses, a woman
scrubbing stains from a shirt. A man sipping coffee
gazes at the newspaper. On the roads, men

tensed and lean as whips hunch over their bikes
headed for the mountains. In cars, women
and children quarrel on their way to the pool.

Rain hits our roof, flows down the steep pitch
into gutters, slips into the grass.

Poem Ending in a Line from Sylvia Plath

Arranged on the table, I close my eyes,
my hand curled around a cylinder
I'm told to squeeze every five seconds.

Stoic and intent, I've answered questions
about disease, travel, intimate relations:
have you had sex with strangers

in Gambia, Nepal—or with possible drug users,
within the last five years,
exchanged needles? I never revealed

my trips south of the border, the tango.
Nor confessed about the Turk
who seized my hand once and told me

he envied my long life ahead.
Nor admitted I've been reading Sylvia Plath
late at night, burnishing her poems

inside my head. Ghastly muse,
she's an eternal thirty
I can no more erase than she could kill

her awful daddy, already dead.
When I'm transfixed by thin blue lines
on yellow paper, when I'm weary, daunted,

she appears: a woman with a luminous smile
and a crisp voice who declares,
the blood blooms clean in you, ruby.

Fishing for Blues

Seconds after our friend spies a flurry of birds
over a turbulence of menhaden and bluefish,

he jockeys the sailboat off its tack
and you snap the fishing rod. A minute's play

and the hook locks itself in the fish's lip. Held up,
a plump yard of bluefish reflects an azure sky.

Rapture, as always, is desire fulfilled,
but how to handle the terror in those flat, black eyes,

the tail tapping its castanets in the bucket?
You still it with a hammer, slit it open.

Over the side with the guts. Its sharp scales wedge
beneath your fingernails and blood splatters your shirt.

All nature is perverse, Darwin says.
Waves slap against the hull, a puff of wind bells up

the sails and channel markers toll
as we slip between bridge stanchions,

our tongues and stomachs saying, *bluefish, dinner.*
But my mind keeps returning to the sheen of blue

as the fish breached the surface of the water,
a flash of sunlight arching its back.

Abecedarium in Praise of Being

Ambulatory again, I ascend the mountain trail, attuned to
bird-calls. A hermit thrush serenades from a thick-branched beech.
Cascading notes correspond, I like to think, to desire or
desire's fulfillment or deft
eagerness to express, to expand the universe

from note to note, with flurries of song.
Gravel under my feet, the ground rutted
hard by sudden mountain storms, hailstones, spring thaw,
ice-melt. I've come for black-eyed Susans, insouciant,
just to the side of the trail where it juts open to a meadow.

Knee-deep among their yellow heads, I
luxuriate in the light bathing them, pray they linger
most of July, best of show among marguerites and yarrow,
nettles and red clover. Butterflies rove from blossom to
obliging blossom, frantic over the choice of flower,

plentiful and savory. Some butterflies are plain white, some
queerly marked in a mosaic of colors, their quest
resembling mine, kinetic energy for its own
sake, as I rejoice in the strength of my knees,
thighs, give thanks for this simple treat of walking.

Unless I'd slipped that day, wrenched my knee, how could I
vouch for the power to heal? Walking, one foot, another,
what a pleasure and wonder, my mountain
Xanadu coming at the ridge where I could dance and sing,
yet no one would hear but the surrounding hills, soft
zephyrs rustling the branches of red pine, poplar, birch.

Aftermath: The Swans

Seven white shadows ripple
and merge as they swim in the estuary
(*across the clear blue face of the sky,*
no jet trails, feathery and white.)
Foraging in the wash of red-brown seaweed,
they tilt their heads and swim
in concert with one another
(*and still the ruins flame and smolder.*)
Pure and white, smug in their plumpness,
their beauty culminates in vanity's
long arched neck.
(*Bodies charred, sirens wailing.*)
Mute, their song is graceful ease of movement,
the steady flap flap of webbed feet
hidden and skillful.
(*across the clear blue face of the sky*
no jet trails, feathery and white.)
Seven white shadows ripple
and merge as they swim.

Warrior One

Maybe it's because my mother swooped down
to touch her toes—showing her stuff to me and my sisters—
legs straight, her smile taunting us
to be smart and flexible.

Maybe it's because the many-mirrored room
where we practice reflects us back as warriors—
though we are women—arms thrust parallel
to the floor as if we were throwing a lance.

Maybe it's because at home some mornings,
Chica is my only witness, rising from sleep,
her back a perfect bow, her paws stretched
forward, rump in the air. I mimic her, my back
a table, then a deep exhale as I arch like a cat.

Maybe it's because I see my mother's smile
as I practice my yoga, mornings at home
or in the many-mirrored room—arms sweeping
skywards then a swan dive to wrap my hands
around my ankles.

Maybe it's simply to exult as I shift to the lunge,
arms thrust overhead, fingertips pointed, until
I begin to quiver, ankle-knee-thigh. Not my mother,
but some other creature I'm coming to know.

About the Author

Claire Keyes grew up in Boston, Massachusetts, the seventh child in an Irish-Catholic family of eight. Parochial schools led to Boston State College, Boston College (M.A.) and the University of Massachusetts (Ph. D.) Professor Emerita at Salem State College, where she taught English for 30 years, she is the author of *The Aesthetics of Power: The Poetry of Adrienne Rich*. Her poems and reviews have appeared in such journals as *Valparaiso Review, Calyx, Blueline*, and *The Women's Review of Books*, as well as in several anthologies, including *Letters to the World, Poems from the Wom-Po Listserv* and *Poems of Exotic Places*. She is a recipient of a grant in poetry from the Massachusetts Cultural Council and a fellowship from the Wurlitzer Foundation in Taos, New Mexico. Her chapbook, *Rising and Falling*, won the Foothills Poetry Competition. She lives in Marblehead, Massachusetts, with her husband, Jay Moore.

Other Recent Titles from Mayapple Press:

Judith Kerman and Amee Schmidt, eds., *Greenhouse: The First 5 Years of the Rustbelt Roethke Writers' Workshop*, 2008
    Paper, 78 pp, $14.95 plus s&h
    ISBN 978-0932412-683
Cati Porter, *Seven Floors Up*, 2008
    Paper, 66 pp, $14.95 plus s&h
    ISBN 978-0932412-676
Rabbi Manes Kogan, *Fables from the Jewish Tradition*, 2008
    Paper, 104 pp, $19.95 plus s&h
    ISBN 978-0932412-669
Joy Gaines-Friedler, *Like Vapor*, 2008
    Paper, 64 pp, $14.95 plus s&h
    ISBN 978-0932412-652
Jane Piirto, *Saunas*, 2008
    Paper, 100 pp, $15.95 plus s&h
    ISBN 978-0932412-645
Joel Thomas Katz, *Away*, 2008
    Paper, 42 pp, $12.95 plus s&h
    ISBN 978-0932412-638
Tenea D. Johnson, *Starting Friction*, 2008
    Paper, 38 pp, $12.95 plus s&h
    ISBN 978-0932412-621
Brian Aldiss, *The Prehistory of Mind*, 2008
    Paper, 76 pp, $14.95 plus s&h
    ISBN 978-0932412-614
Andy Christ, *Philip and the Poet*, 2008
    Paper, 26 pp, $12.95 plus s&h
    ISBN 978-0932412-607
Jayne Pupek, *Forms of Intercession*, 2008
    Paper, 102 pp, $15.95 plus s&h
    ISBN 978-0932412-591
Elizabeth Kerlikowske, *Dominant Hand*, 2008
    Paper, 64 pp, $14.95 plus s&h
    ISBN 978-0932412-584
Marilyn Jurich, *Defying the Eye Chart*, 2008
    Paper, 120 pp, $15.95 plus s&h
    ISBN 978-0932412-577

For a complete catalog of Mayapple Press publications, please visit our website at *www.mayapplepress.com*. Books can be ordered direct from our website with secure on-line payment using PayPal, or by mail (check or money order). Or order through your local bookseller.